T0345843

INSTITUTE OF CONTEMPORARY ART (ICA)
BOSTON

DILLER SCOFIDIO + RENFRO

INSTITUTE OF CONTEMPORARY ART (ICA)
BOSTON

Photographic essay by Iwan Baan

Ediciones Polígrafa

© **of this edition**: Ediciones Polígrafa, Barcelona, 2011
Balmes, 54. 08007 Barcelona
www.edicionespoligrafa.com

© **of the photographs and texts**: the authors

Photographic credits: Iwan Baan (except pp. 16–31, courtesy of
Diller Scofidio + Renfro)

Concept of the Collection: Francisco Rei
Coordination: Inés García Fernández
Copy Editor: Richard G. Gallin
Design: mot (www.motstudio.com)
Page layout: Estudi Polígrafa / Carlos J. Santos
Color separation: Estudi Polígrafa / Annel Biu
Printing and binding: Novoprint, Barcelona

Available in USA and Canada through
D.A.P. /Distributed Art Publishers
155 Sixth Avenue, 2nd Floor, New York, N.Y. 10013
Tel. (212) 627-1999; Fax: (212) 627-9484

ISBN: 978-84-343-1280-7
Dep. legal: B. 25.673 - 2011

Back cover: Excerpt of Project Memory by Diller Scofidio +
Renfro, pp. 72–73 of this publication.

CONTENTS

Northeast view of the
Institute of Contemporary
Art (ICA), Boston
Photo: Iwan Baan

The HarborWalk
and public grandstand
Photo: Iwan Baan

When it opened in December 2006, the Institute of Contemporary Art / Boston was the first new art museum to be built here in nearly a century. Diller + Scofidio's design — now Diller Scofidio + Renfro — brought progressive architecture to Boston, changing not just the museum, but the seaport and the city.

Boston is a small and vibrant city. With a population of just 617,000 within the city limits, it still retains the pride of former centuries when known as the Athens of America, it was home to writers, artists, activists, abolitionists, merchants, and political leaders. This reverence for the past has led, however, to a city resistant to architectural change and a predisposition to historical and contextual references. With few exceptions (I. M. Pei & Partners' John Hancock Tower and Paul Rudolph's City Hall and some significant contemporary campus landmarks — mostly in Cambridge), architecture in Boston has not kept pace with the innovative work of the city in higher education, technology, and life sciences.

The Institute of Contemporary Art's location on a small parcel of land on the shores of Boston Harbor dictated both its architectural opportunities and its limitations. Facing north, the building reveals an array of urban vistas: the skyline of Boston's Financial District, historic steel bridges, the airport, the working ports, and the piers and neighborhoods of East Boston — all seen within the realm of water and sky. As with the contemporary art inside, it is a view in constant flux. The changing New England weather palpably occupies important museum spaces just as the long-awaited development of the seaport district will continue to modify its urban context.

When the ICA selected Diller + Scofidio as architects for our new museum, the challenges, risks, and possibilities were clear and plentiful. We charged them with designing a museum that would serve as both a civic and a cultural institution, one whose presence would shape the waterfront. We asked them to maximize the waterfront location without sacrificing the visitors' encounters with the art and artists within; we needed a flexible facility for both the visual and the performing arts; and we wanted a technologically sophisticated building, yet one that would stand the test of time and have the affection of Bostonians for generations to come. All this would need to be accomplished in the context of a tight site footprint, a small budget, and a city known for difficult permitting and regulatory procedures.

The ICA's decision to hire Diller + Scofidio reflected our belief in the firm's vision that architecture can shape as well as reflect contemporary experience. We were appreciative of their collaborative spirit and the extraordinary intelligence, passion, and imagination they had demonstrated in their earlier, albeit mostly unbuilt, work. We were looking for a firm that would embrace a strong client and whose career trajectory augured well for an innovative breakthrough building.

The conceptual rigor, artistic vision, and passion Diller + Scofidio brought to the project is clearly evident upon approaching the ICA and entering the two-story lobby where the key design concepts of "conceal and reveal" unfold throughout. It is a lean, four-story building, open and civic from the ground up, ending in the galleries on the top floor, where a more private and contemplative series of experiences is shaped.

The glass elevator serves passengers and freight and offers unexpected glimpses of the harbor as it slowly travels upward. The back and side of the stage in the theater are glass walls that can be shaded for more traditional theatrical presentations or opened to engage the sights and movements of the outer world. A learning lab "mediatheque" functions as the museum's "hearth" with its unusual, horizonless water view, the equivalent of the fire in the fireplace. A fourth-floor gallery spanning the width of the building connects galleries for temporary exhibitions with those for the ICA Collection and reveals the full panoramic view of the city and harbor.

Many of these spaces and their visual and experiential impact are created by a 75-foot cantilever that ends at the water's edge, defining an outdoor room that increases the museum's footprint and programming space, extending the line and warmth of the wood floor and ceiling of the theater to the exterior plaza, and enabling the ICA to place all its galleries on the top floor with skylights and scrims designed to capture the northern light.

When the new ICA opened, it was the 25th location for the museum in its 75-year history and its first, permanent, freestanding home. In our first five years here, we've worked with more than 1,000 artists and welcomed more than 1,000,000 visitors who have witnessed extraordinary works of art and important artistic experimentation. Each year, more than 12,000 teens and families participate in ICA programs, demonstrating the power of art and museums to open minds and change lives. Our exhibitions, collections, and performances help us better serve our core institutional mission of fostering the knowledge, creativity, and curiosity that we believe are enriched by a sustained engagement with the art of our time. Our new museum gave all of these aspirations a home.

Diller + Scofidio's balanced use of cool and transparent glass with the warmth of wood and the energy of light, as well as their design of spare, flexible spaces for presenting contemporary art, was a revelation for a city and an architectural community that had awaited the building's highly anticipated completion. The transformation of the ICA, the waterfront, and the city was a dramatic change, symbolizing a city embracing the future. Diller Scofidio + Renfro immediately went on to design equally iconic landmarks including the High Line and Alice Tully Hall in New York. Their brilliant and beautiful design of the ICA was a harbinger of change: edgy, bold, and breathtaking, transforming the landscape for contemporary art and culture in Boston and for the artists, art, and ideas of our time.

Jill Medvedow
Director
ICA/Boston

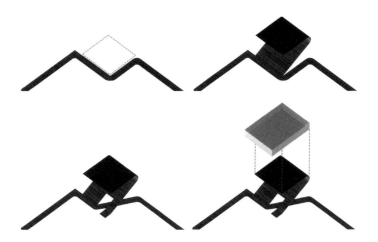

As in any creative field, the architect must reconcile his or her background and experience with the cultural reality of their time. Would you tell us about your training?

Liz attended the Cooper Union School of Art and received a Bachelor of Architecture from the Cooper Union School of Architecture. Ric studied at the Cooper Union School of Architecture and received a Bachelor of Architecture degree from Columbia University. Charles attended Rice University and received a Master of Architecture degree from Columbia University.

How would you characterize the relationship of your work to the museum?

We constantly find ourselves on either side of the museum wall, having played the role of artists, curators, exhibition designers, and now the role of architect at the ICA, having to speak in the voice of the institution. We've essentially been the user group of the building and have developed a great deal of empathy for the constituencies of the museum. We believe that much like the museum, architecture has a responsibility to raise the consciousness of the public.

As distinct from other typologies, the architectural conception of a museum must take into account the critical presence of the artwork. Do you regard this dialectical confrontation between the two practices as an added difficulty?

No. We began the project with the assumption that architecture would neither compete with the art nor be a neutral backdrop. Just as the museum takes on the role of educating, delighting, and challenging its public through the artwork it chooses to display, architecture has the responsibility of educating, delighting, and challenging its public through space. There is no reason the museum building and its content should be anything but creative partners.

Your work straddles both art and architecture. Do you define your projects as one or the other?

We have never needed the clarity of our work being categorized as either "art" or "architecture." We are defined by a particular in-between-ness, a middle ground that is contaminated from all sides. If there is a common thread across our work, it might be our desire to interfere with spatial conventions of the everyday, whose familiarity inoculates us from developing new cultural understandings.

What have been your referents?

Duchamp, Foucault, Venturi and Scott Brown, Walter Benjamin, Gordon Matta-Clark, Robert Smithson, Dan Graham, Chris Burden, Vito Acconci, Philip Glass, Glenn Gould, Stanley Kubrick, Wooster Group... literature, film, pop culture, mad science, mapping, fashion, pulp fiction, automobiles, gastronomy... perhaps, everything but architecture.

Is there a particular one that has had a direct impact on your own interdisciplinary practice?

Duchamp. He broke disciplinary boundaries; he didn't belong in any particular discipline or time frame. His indeterminacy permeated everything, and he was critical of establishments: cultural and social, spanning from the museum to the market. He broke disciplinary boundaries between painting, sculpture, and installation art, and redefined the terms of spectatorship. But maybe the most important aspect of his work was his parallel play of visual and textual languages.

The importance of context has become a commonplace in architectural thinking in recent decades. Has the building's position on the waterfront determined the project?

The waterfront site had a tremendous effect on the building's design. The Boston waterfront is both a great asset for the museum and a distraction from its inwardly focused program, so we designed the ICA as an apparatus for producing and re-producing ways of mediating its surrounding waterfront site. The building essentially analyzes the view and regulates the experience of the harbor over time, distributing it in a controlled manner. The views of the harbor are always partial and fleeting; they follow you and hide from you.

Study models
Photo: Courtesy of Diller
Scofidio + Renfro

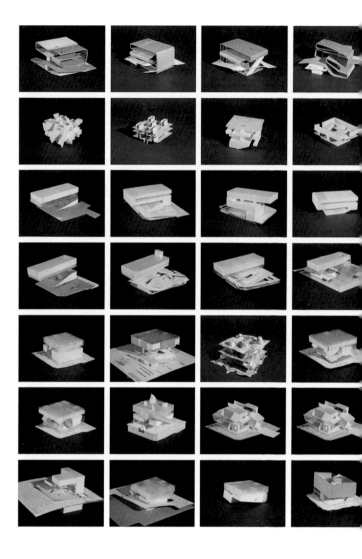

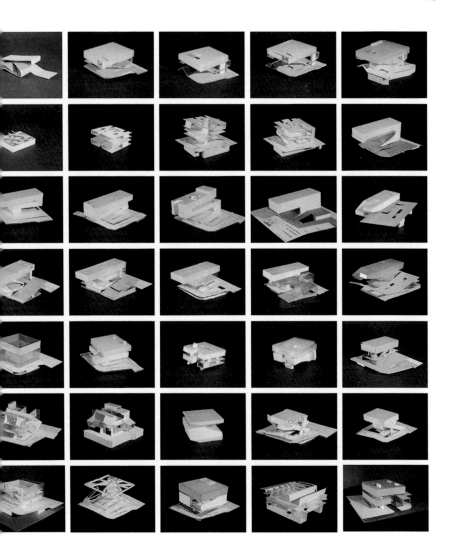

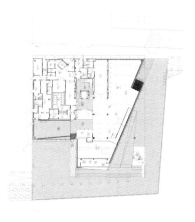

Ground-floor plan
First-floor plan

5   10   20

meters

N

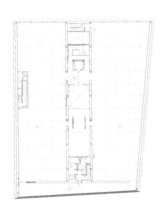

Second-floor plan
Third-floor plan

5   10   20

meters

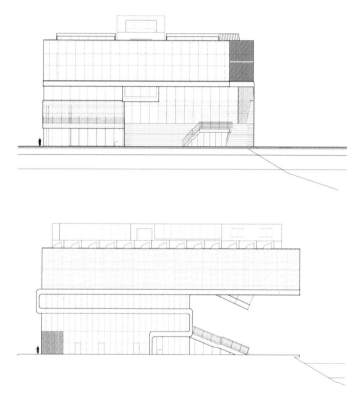

North Elevation
East Elevation

5   10   20

meters

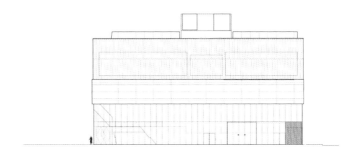

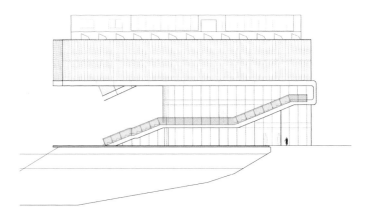

South Elevation
West Elevation

5   10   20

meters

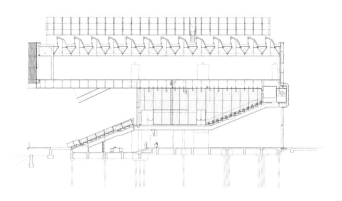

Sections of the building

One of the most surprising images of the ICA shows a media room with the window over-looking the sea at the rear. Does technology still play an important role in your work?

We believe architecture is technology. If by technology you mean digital, we believe that architecture's smallest units are bricks and pixels. But technology is only a means to an end, a tool to enhance space making. Common to all of our work is the opening of architecture to new technologies in which "smart" and "dumb" systems can find new relations. This includes sustainable systems, the exploration of new materials even from unlikely sources such as aerospace and medicine, and the use of traditional materials in new ways.

After the Second World War museum architecture took a markedly iconic turn (Wright, Niemeyer. . .) which seems to be accentuated in the latest generation of museums. Where would you situate your own experience?

For us, a museum, a theater stage, an urban space, even an empty suburban lot is never a tabula rasa for a formal experiment; it is a site encoded with rules of organization and conduct that must be interrogated before an intervention can take place. Our work attempts to interrupt those conventions and find new architectural expressions for a culture in flux. We do not begin the design process by focusing on image or form.

In a museum the light is obviously very important. To what extent has the proposed treatment affected the form of the building?

We often say the building is built from the ground up for the public spaces and the sky down for the private, more contemplative gallery spaces, which have direct ac-cess to diffused and controlled light. The form of the building comes in part from an effort to intertwine this museum space with civic space. The HarborWalk threads its way through the museum's ground floor; it's stretched into a public grandstand and follows the contours of the museum's public spaces until it finally becomes the platform that holds the gallery in the sky.

Building under construction
Photo: Courtesy of Diller
Scofidio + Renfro

What particular features of the proposed circulation plan should we focus on?

Circulation throughout the museum is choreographed to reveal the site in controlled doses. As visitors enter the building, the Boston Harbor view is compressed in the lobby, then scanned vertically by the glass elevator, manipulated in theatrical performances, denied in the galleries, revealed as a panorama at the north gallery crossover, and edited to only the texture of water at the mediatheque.

And the museological program: to what extent has it determined the project?

We worked closely with the ICA's director and curators to develop area and adjacency requirements for the ICA's program. Working on a small site with the desire to top light the gallery spaces, we were able to place the expansive gallery on a single level by cantilevering the gallery into city-owned property which was transferred to the ICA in exchange for the creation of a new harbor-facing plaza underneath. The resulting cantilevered floor and the HarborWalk below provide the primary image of the building.

A building designed to host a contemporary art collection and exhibition program must take into account both the increasing presence of new technologies and the exhibition's requirements: enclosed spaces, soundproofing, darkness. . . . Do you consider these needs are fully covered?

Yes. A strategy of permanent flexibility permeates the major program requirements of both the galleries and theater space. In the galleries, a grid with electric and structural nodes allows temporary or semipermanent walls of varying heights to be effortlessly constructed. Walls can be built to the ceiling and black-out shades can be deployed for media pieces sensitive to light. The glass walls on the north and west sides of the theater can be visually and acoustically controlled to accommodate performance types ranging from live music and dance to film and presentations.

Until very recently, the museum was regarded as a space for reflection and contemplation, the locus of aesthetic experience — with all of the mystical resonances that might be ascribed to it. Now, however, it forms part of a dynamic of consumption which the architecture must obviously take into consideration.

We have to be vigilant about our institutions. We have to constantly look out for their interests. Sometimes it takes stealthy, undercover work, to be able to be part of them but also to not let them go the course that they would go naturally.

And finally, with the construction of the building and the conditioning of the surrounding area completed, has it turned out as you expected? How has it been received?

The ICA was the first building to be constructed on Fan Pier, a former industrial district on Boston Harbor being transformed into a high-density, mixed-use development. As such, we intended the ICA to act as a landmark and catalyst for future development while anticipating a context that would change from parking lots to a dense urban fabric. Since the ICA's completion, it has enjoyed tremendous success; it has been embraced by both the general public and the press and has acted as a catalyst for redevelopment and revitalization in South Boston. It also catalyzed a somewhat dormant contemporary art audience in Boston. ICA now plays in the international arena of contemporary art institutions and has experienced a tenfold increase in visitorship.

PHOTOGRAPHIC ESSAY

Iwan Baan

The Institute of Contemporary Art (ICA) is the first new museum to be built in Boston in 100 years. The design negotiates between two competing objectives: to perform as a dynamic civic building for public and social activities, and as a controlled, contemplative atmosphere for the appreciation of contemporary art. The "public" building is thus built from the ground up; the "intimate" building, from the sky down.

The Boston HarborWalk, a 47-mile-long public walkway, borders the northern and western edges of the ICA site. The marine grade wood surface of the walkway — a democratic space that belongs to the citizens of Boston — is extended into the new building as a primary architectural element. The HarborWalk becomes a pliable wrapper that defines the building's major public spaces. It folds up from the walkway into a grandstand facing the water and flattens to form a stage; it then turns up to form raked theater seating and seamlessly envelopes the theater space; it ultimately slips out through the glass skin to produce the ceiling of the exterior public "room." This ambiguous surface moves from exterior into interior, transforming public into semipublic space. Above the wrapper sits the gallery volume: a large exhibition space on one level that dramatically cantilevers over the HarborWalk toward the water.

The cantilevered exhibition space extends into city-owned property, which was transferred to the ICA in exchange for the creation of the new covered public "room" below. The exhibition space was designed as a flexible, column-free volume 16 feet tall, partitioned into east and west galleries by the central core. The exhibition space is easily transformed from open galleries to intimate rooms for the presentation of art ranging from large scale three-dimensional work to sound— and light-sensitive video. For these purposes, Diller Scofidio + Renfro developed a system of parallel technical tracks within the scrim ceiling containing lighting, electric, air, sprinklers, security, data and structural hanging nodes. A corresponding grid on the floor with electric and structural nodes allows temporary or semipermanent walls of varying heights to be effortlessly constructed. Uniform, diffused daylight is brought into the gallery level through a series of north-facing light monitors and controlled through an automated roll-down shade system, allowing for varying degrees of lightness or total blackout depending on the show.

The 330-seat multipurpose theater is fully glazed on its north and west faces, allowing the harbor view to become the backdrop for the stage. Flexibility was of paramount importance for the theater, which presents a variety of live performance types and must often change between three functions in the course of a day. The glass walls on the north and west walls can be visually and acoustically controlled to accommodate performance types ranging from live music and dance to film and other presentations. Variable acoustic panels can be deployed at the touch of a button to change the acoustics from reflective to absorbent. Blackout shades and scrim shades can be deployed to block or veil views to the outside and to eliminate unwanted daylight.

The mediatheque — a digital media gallery and reading area — is suspended from the underside of the cantilevered exhibition volume and accessed from above. This stepped space frames only the water and denies any view of its foreground — the land. The mediatheque is equipped with computer stations with online access and fed by a central server providing a growing database of digital artworks.

The passage through the ICA is choreographed to dispense the view of Boston's harbor in small controlled doses. Upon entry, the view is compressed under the belly of the theater, then scanned by the glass elevator, used as a variable backdrop in the theater, denied entirely in the galleries, and revealed as a panorama at the crossover gallery. At the glass wall of the digital media gallery suspended beneath the cantilever, the harbor context is highly edited to frame only the mesmerizing texture of water. A tranquil natural/electronic atmosphere highlights every nuance of weather change and shift of light as the day progresses.

Diller Scofidio + Renfro

Project
Institute of Contemporary Art (ICA), Boston
Client
Institute of Contemporary Art (ICA), Boston
Address
100 Northern Avenue
Boston, Massachusetts 02210
Lead Design
Diller Scofidio + Renfro
Principals
Elizabeth Diller
Ricardo Scofidio
Charles Renfro
Project Team
Jesse Saylor
Flavio Stigliano
Deane Simpson
Eric Howeler
Associate Architects
Perry Dean Rogers and Partners, Boston MA
Associate Architects Project Team
Martha Pilgreen, Principal in Charge
Gregory C. Burchard, Mike Waters, Project Manager
Henry Scollard, Project Designer
Project Management
Seamus Henchy Associates
Skanska USA
Planning
Design Start: 2001
Construction Start: 2004
Completion Date: 2006
Size
6,038.69 square meters.
Building Contractor
George B. H. Macomber Company
Skanska USA

Budget
$ 41,5 million
Financing
Institute of Contemporary Art Provided in part by the Massachusetts Development Finance Agency.
Program
The 6,038.69 square meters building on Boston Harbor includes 1,672.25 square meters of galleries, curatorial and conservation spaces, a café/restaurant, a bookstore, education/workshop facilities, administrative offices, and a 330-seat performing arts space for music, film, theater, and dance.
Consultants
SMEP: Arup New York, Markus Schulte
Theater Consultants: Fisher Dachs
Acoustics: Jaffe Holden Acoustics
Project Management: Seamus Henchy Associates
Lighting: Arup London, Andy Sedgewick

SELECT BIBLIOGRAPHY

Monographs

_Brooke Hodge, *et al.*, *Skin + Bones: Parallel Practices in Fashion and Architecture*, New York: Thames and Hudson, 2006, pp. 80-87.

_Guido Inercet, *et al.*, *Diller + Scofidio (+Renfro): The Ciliary Function, Works and Projects 1979-2007*, Milan: Skira, 2007.

_Nicholas Baume, "It's Still Fun to Have Architecture: Interview with Diller Scofidio + Renfro," *Super Vision*, Cambridge MA: MIT Press, 2006, pp. 178-91.

Journals and Periodical Literature

_Sarah Amelar, "Diller Scofidio + Renfro Fold the ICA into Boston's Waterfront," *Architectural Record*, March 2007, pp. 108-15.

_"Art and the City," *Boston Globe*, April 23, 2006, p. E8.

_Geraldine Baum, "Diller and Scofidio, in the business of architecture and artistry," *Los Angeles Times,* December 12, 2010.

_Raul Barreneche, "Critical Mass," *Travel + Leisure*, March 2007, pp. 140-42.

_Harvey Blume, "Q&A with Elizabeth Diller," *Boston Globe,* February 18, 2007.

_Michele Calzavara, "Diller Scofidio + Renfro. ICA, Boston," *Abitare,* February 2007, pp. 122-29.

_Robert Campbell, "Designers' Plans for New ICA Reflect Changing Landscape," *Boston Sunday Globe*, August 26, 2001, p. 5.

___."Alone on the Waterfront in South Boston: the Unfinished ICA is a Bold Presence," *Boston Globe*, May 28, 2006, p. 3.

___."New ICA building emerges into the light," *Boston Globe*, November 30, 2006.

___."New ICA building emerges into the light," *International Herald Tribune*, November 30, 2006.

___."A Vision Fulfilled at Harbor's Edge," *Boston Globe*, December 1, 2006.

___."A floating palace for art," *Boston Globe*, December 6, 2006.

___."By standing out: it's a perfect fit," *Boston Globe*, December 10, 2006.

___."Another museum that's a work of art," *Boston Globe*, January 13, 2008.

_Brian Carter, "Harbour Master," *Architectural Review*, February 2007, pp. 40-51.

_Justin Davidson, "The Illusionists," *New Yorker,* May 14, 2007, pp. 126-37.

_Tom Dyckhoff, "Boston's New Gallery is a Real Tease," *Times,* December 12, 2006.

_Hal Foster, "Architecture-Eye," *Art Forum,* February 2007, pp. 246-53.

_Christopher Hawthorne, "Flood of Ideas on Boston Harbor," *Los Angeles Times,* December 11, 2006.

_Ada Louise Huxtable, "The Hub of Architecture: Boston and a Neighbor Embrace the New With Fervor," *Wall Street Journal,* July 31, 2003, p. D8.

_"Institute of Contemporary Art /Boston," *A+U,* July 2005, pp. 76-85.

_Philip Kennicott, "Museum Sticks Its Neck Out–But Only So Far," *Washington Post,* December 24, 2006.

_Richard Lacayo, "First Thinking Then Building," *Time Magazine,* December 4, 2006.

_Nancy Levinson, "View Masters," *I.D,* March - April 2007, pp. 91-92.

_Arthur Lubow, "Architects, in Theory," *New York Times Magazine,* February 16, 2003, pp. 36-41.

_Todd MacDonough, "Education of the Senses," *Art in America,* March 2007, pp. 122-27.

_Gerhard Mack, "Im Treibhaus der Avantgarde," *Art,* January 2008, pp. 44-51.

_Vernon Mays, "The Art of Building for Art," *Architect,* March 2007, pp. 72-79.

_Justin McGuirk, "Home Turf: Diller Scofidio + Renfro," *Art Review,* September 2006.

_Cate McQuaid, "The New ICA," *Boston Globe,* December 6, 2006, pp. K1-9.

_Bill Millard, "Boston's First New Museum in a Century," *Icon,* February 2007, pp. 66-72.

_Herbert Muschamp, "For All You Observers of the Urban Extravaganza," *New York Times,* November 10, late ed. 2002, p. AR34.

_Hans Ulrich Obrist, "The Outsiders: Elizabeth Diller, Ricardo Scofidio and Charles Renfro," *DAMn,* June-July 2008, no. 17, pp. 112-18.

_Nicolai Ouroussoff, "Expansive Vistas Both Inside and Out," *New York Times,* December 6, 2006.

___."Expansive Vistas Both Inside and Out," *AV Monographs,* 2006, pp. 5-15.

_David Rockwell, "The Time 100: Architects: Elizabeth Diller and Ricardo Scofidio," *Time Magazine,* May 11, 2009, p. 95.

_Jessie Scanlon, "Boston Pops," *Dwell,* October 2007, pp. 236-50.

_Hilarie M. Sheets, "Pathology Pathologically? Optimistic," *ARTnews,* September 2006, pp. 60-62.

_Michael Silverberg, "High Visibility," *Metropolis,* September 2006, pp. 42.

_Rachel Strutt, "The Visionary," *Boston Globe,* December 31, 2006.

_Christine Temin, "Waterfront Colors: Boston's Modern Update," *Washington Post,* December 8, 2006.

_"The Institute of Contemporary Art," *Detail,* March 2007, pp. 32-41.

_Mika Yoshida and David G. Imber, "A Jewel on Boston Harbor," *Casa Brutus 86,* May 2007, pp. 182-83.

_Mimi Zeiger, "Now on View," *Architecture,* September 2006, pp. 68-77.